Music Minus One

WORLD FAVORITES
Music Minus One Clarinet, Beginning Level

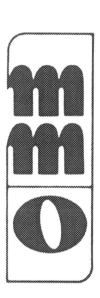

Music Minus One Clarinet

WORLD FAVORITES
- beginning level -

*Forty-one selections from around the world,
chosen for their beauty and ease of performance.
Certain to delight the beginning student.
(1st-3rd year ability)*

3244

IN THE GOOD OLD SUMMER TIME

4 bar piano intro
precedes solo.

GEORGE EVANS

Tempo di Valse

3244

MY WILD IRISH ROSE

4 bar piano intro
precedes solo.

CHAUNCEY OLCOTT

Tempo di Valse

SWEET MOLLY MALONE

8 bar piano intro
precedes solo.

Allegretto

IRISH SONG

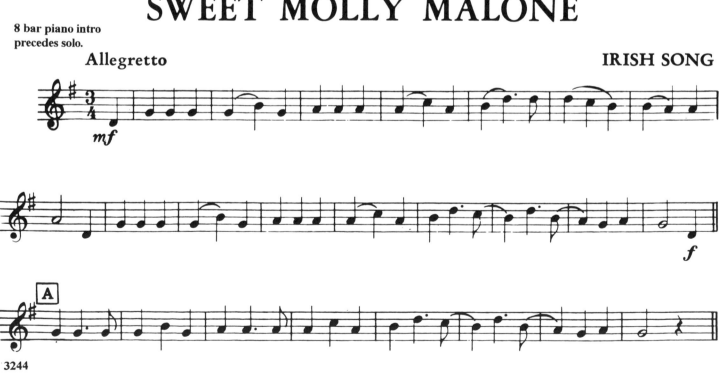

TO A WILD ROSE

4 bar piano intro
precedes solo.

EDWARD A. MACDOWELL

THE YELLOW ROSE OF TEXAS

Brightly

COWBOY SONG

3244

BECAUSE

GUY D'HARDELOT

PANIS ANGELICUS

2 bar piano intro
precedes solo.

CESAR FRANCK

GLOW WORM

2 bar piano intro
precedes solo.

PAUL LINCKE

ETUDE

3/4 bar piano intro
precedes solo.

FREDERIC CHOPIN, Op. 10, No. 3

Poco lento

mp

LONDONDERRY AIR

2 ½ bar piano intro
precedes solo.

IRISH MELODY

Moderato

mp

3244

Black Is The Color Of My True Love's Hair

2 bar piano intro
precedes solo.

Slowly

FOLK SONG

GREENSLEEVES

1 2/3 bar piano intro
precedes solo.

Moderato

ENGLISH FOLK SONG

DEEP RIVER

2 bar piano intro
precedes solo.

SPIRITUAL

RED RIVER VALLEY

3/4 bar piano intro
precedes solo.

TRADITIONAL

MIGHTY LAK' A ROSE

2 bar piano intro
precedes solo.

ETHELBERT NEVIN

Slowly, with expression

TO A WATER LILY

EDWARD A. MACDOWELL

2 bar piano intro
precedes solo

Dreamy

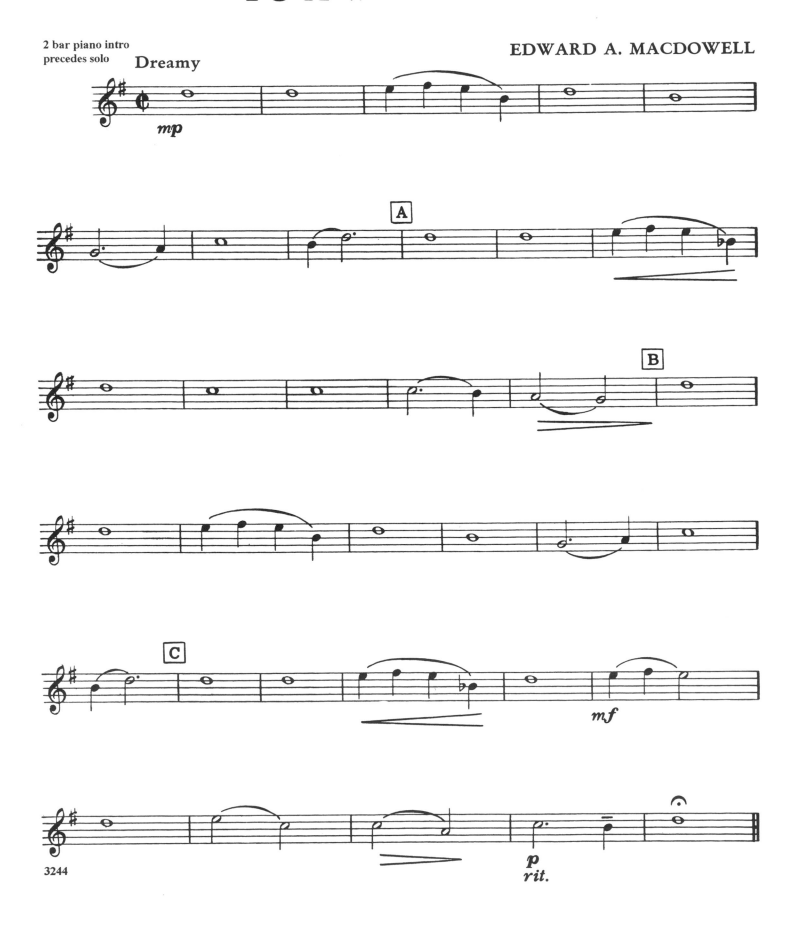

3244

CHICKEN REEL

Moderato

JOSEPH M. DALY

THE BIRTHDAY OF A KING

2 bar piano intro
precedes solo.

W. H. NEIDLINGER

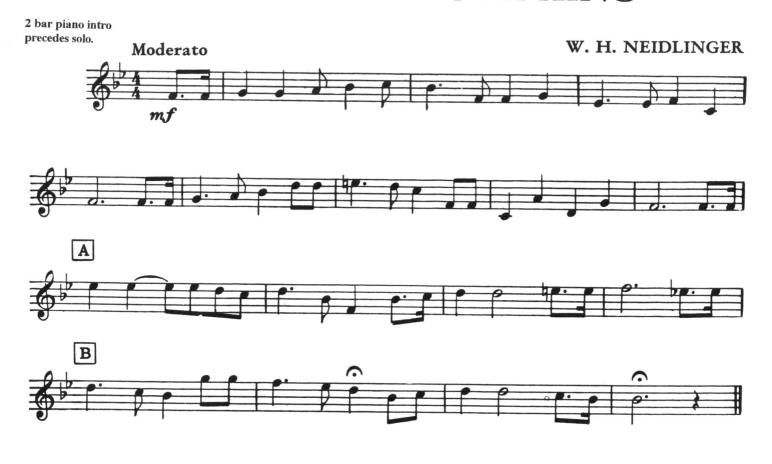

NEARER, MY GOD, TO THEE

2 bar piano intro
precedes solo.

LOWELL MASON

3244

He's Got The Whole World In His Hands

Moderato

TRADITIONAL

PARADE OF THE TIN SOLDIERS

LEON JESSEL

2 bar piano intro
precedes solo.

3244

THE MARINES' HYMN

March tempo

U. S. MARINE CORPS SONG

CAISSON SONG

U. S. ARMY SONG

ON THE BANKS OF THE WABASH

PAUL DRESSER

3244

FLOW GENTLY, SWEET AFTON

J. E. SPILMAN

CLAIR DE LUNE

1 bar piano intro
precedes solo.

CLAUDE DEBUSSY

Andante expressivo

rit.

3244

FASCINATION

F. D. MARCHETTI

TESORO MIO

E. BECUCCI

STAR OF THE EAST

2 bar piano intro
precedes solo.

Moderato

AMANDA KENNEDY

AURA LEE

Moderato

GEORGE POULTON

THEN YOU'LL REMEMBER ME

Andante

2 3/4 bar piano intro
precedes solo.

M. W. BALFE

7098

MEDLEY OF CHRISTMAS CAROLS
WE THREE KINGS OF ORIENT ARE

JOHN H. HOPKINS

4 bar piano intro
precedes solo.

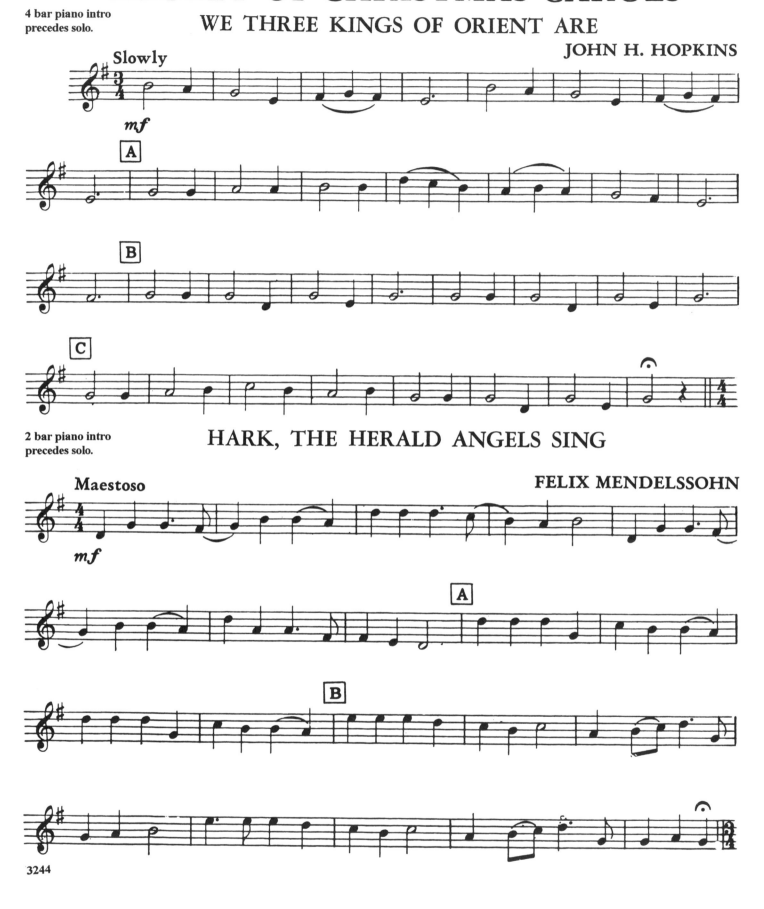

2 bar piano intro
precedes solo.

HARK, THE HERALD ANGELS SING

FELIX MENDELSSOHN

AWAY IN A MANGER

JAMES R. MURRAY

2 beats piano intro
precedes solo.

Moderato

mf

A

SILENT NIGHT

FRANZ GRUBER

Moderato

A

p

B

O COME ALL YE FAITHFUL

1 3/4 bar piano intro
precedes solo.

J. READING

Joyously

f

A

B

p

3244

mf

f

rit.

LA PALOMA

SEBASTIAN YRADIER

O SOLE MIO

EDUARDO DI CAPUA

3244

ROMANY LIFE

2 bar piano intro
precedes solo.

VICTOR HERBERT

Allegro

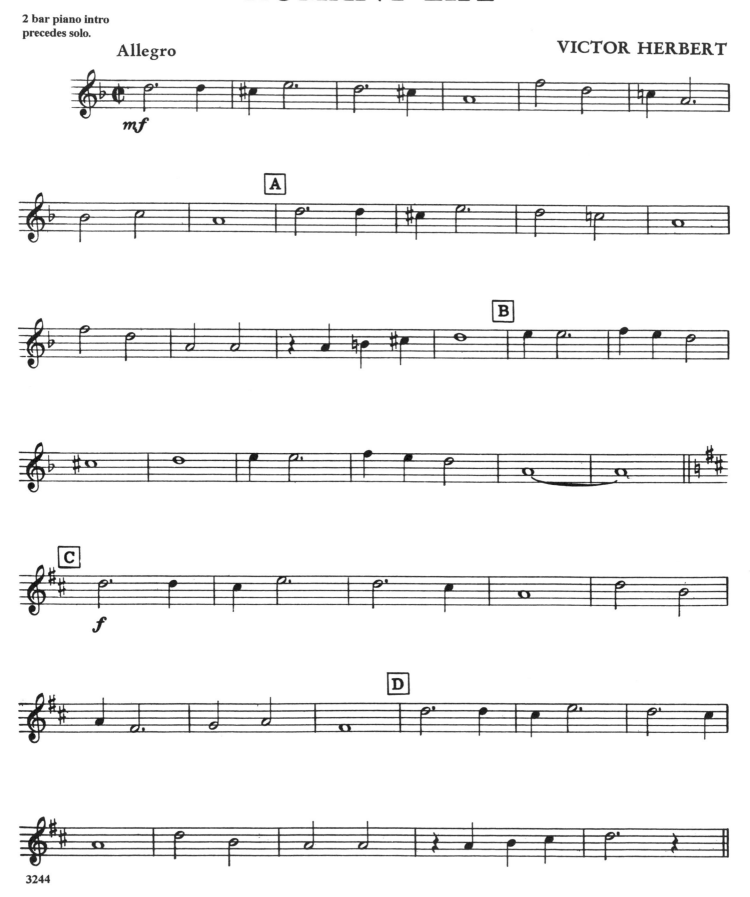

BLUE BELLS OF SCOTLAND

**1 3/4 bar piano intro
precedes solo.**

SCOTCH SONG

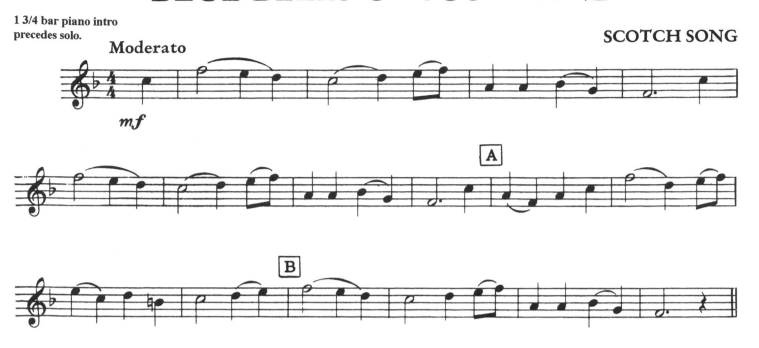

ALL THROUGH THE NIGHT

**2 bar piano intro
precedes solo.**

WELSH SONG

MERRY WIDOW WALTZ

**8 bar piano intro
precedes solo.**

FRANZ LEHAR

3244

Music Minus One Clarinet

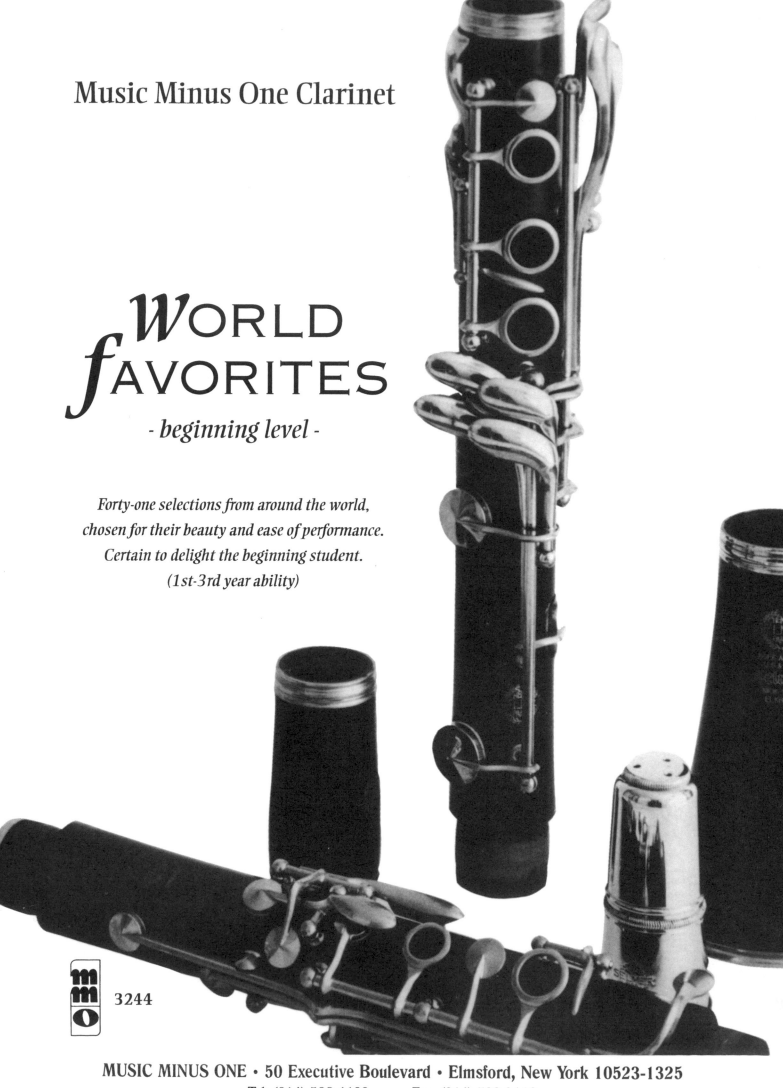

*W*ORLD
*f*AVORITES
- *beginning level* -

Forty-one selections from around the world,
chosen for their beauty and ease of performance.
Certain to delight the beginning student.
(1st-3rd year ability)

3244

MUSIC MINUS ONE • 50 Executive Boulevard • Elmsford, New York 10523-1325
Tel: (914) 592-1188   Fax: (914) 592-3116
E-mail: mmomus@aol.com   Websites: www.minusone.com *and* www.pocketsongs.com